MATH ACTIVITIES

FUN WITH MULTIPLICATION

Lorenzo McLellan
Illustrated by Natasha Rimmington

WINDMILL BOOKS

Published in 2020 by Windmill Books,
an Imprint of Rosen Publishing
29 East 21st Street, New York, NY 10010

Written by Lorenzo McLellan
Illustrated by Natasha Rimmington
Designed by Well Nice, Elaine Wilkinson
Edited by Sebastian Rydberg, Julia Adams

Cataloging-in-Publication Data

Names: McLellan, Lorenzo.
Title: Fun with multiplication / Lorenzo McLellan.
Description: New York : Windmill Books, 2020. | Series: Math activities
Identifiers: ISBN 9781725395312 (pbk.) | ISBN 9781725395336 (library bound) | ISBN 9781725395329 (6 pack)
Subjects: LCSH: Multiplication–Juvenile literature. | Arithmetic–Juvenile literature.
Classification: LCC QA115.M354 2020 | DDC 513.2'13–dc23

Manufactured in the United States of America

CPSIA Compliance Information: Batch BW20WM: For Further Information contact Rosen Publishing, New York, New York at 1-800-237-9932

How to Use This Book

Welcome to the world of Math Activities! This book is filled with times tables facts to help you learn the basics of multiplying—all while having fun! Grab a pencil and some paper so you can write down all your answers... then check your work on pages 30 and 31.

Read about each new topic before you dive into the activities.

Test your knowledge with exciting activities throughout.

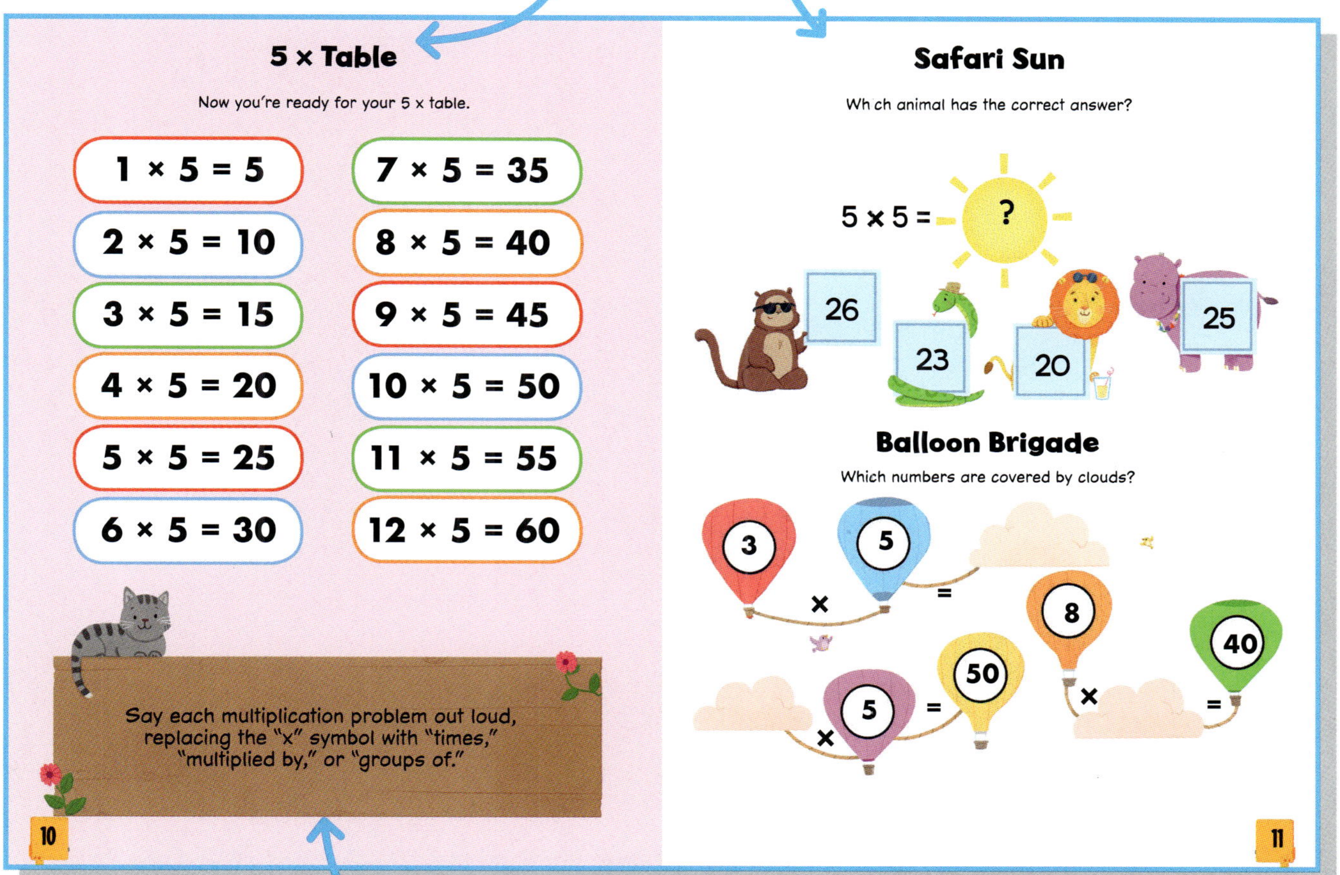

5 × Table

Now you're ready for your 5 x table.

1 × 5 = 5	7 × 5 = 35
2 × 5 = 10	8 × 5 = 40
3 × 5 = 15	9 × 5 = 45
4 × 5 = 20	10 × 5 = 50
5 × 5 = 25	11 × 5 = 55
6 × 5 = 30	12 × 5 = 60

Say each multiplication problem out loud, replacing the "x" symbol with "times," "multiplied by," or "groups of."

10

Safari Sun

Wh ch animal has the correct answer?

Balloon Brigade

Which numbers are covered by clouds?

11

All new topics come with practice activities to learn key skills.

Learn the Symbols (× =)

To start multiplying, these are the symbols you'll need to know.

X — "TIMES," "MULTIPLIED BY," OR "GROUPS OF"

= — "IS EQUAL TO"

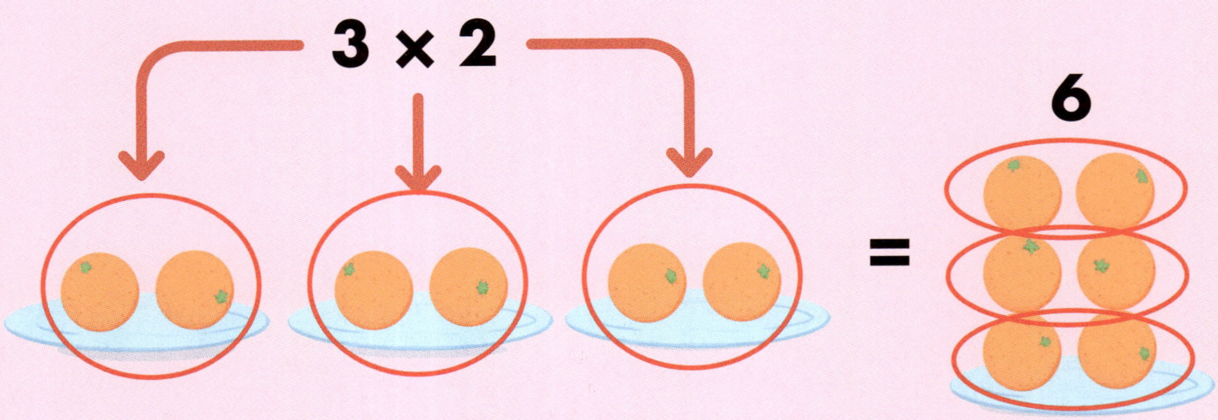

We have 3 **groups of** 2 oranges, which is equal to 6 oranges. 3 **multiplied by** 2 **is equal to** 6.

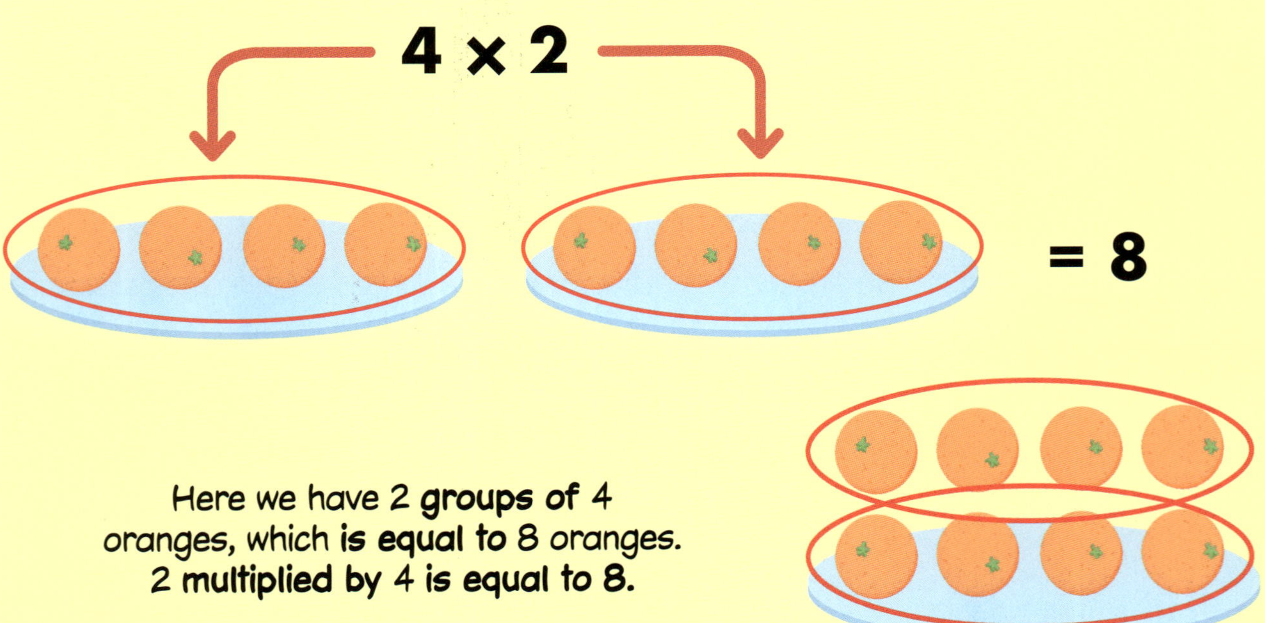

Here we have 2 **groups of** 4 oranges, which **is equal to** 8 oranges. 2 **multiplied by** 4 **is equal to** 8.

Pick the correct symbols to make the number sentence.

4 ? 2 ? 8

× or =

3 ? 2 ? 6

× or =

Machine Mix-up

Help the robot sort the words and phrases into the correct operation machine.

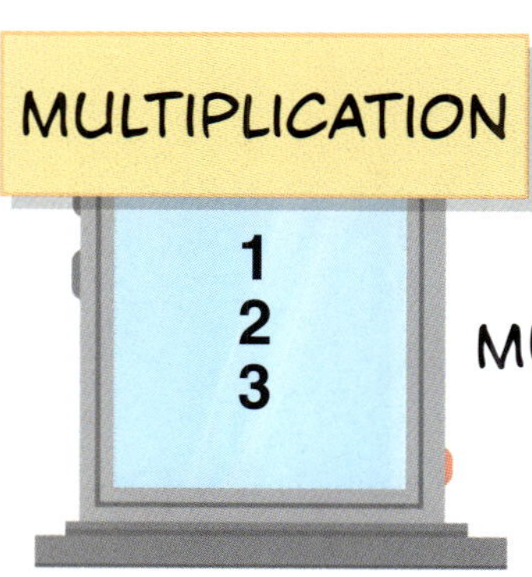

DIVIDED BY

MINUS

MULTIPLIED BY

PLUS

GROUPS OF

TIMES

10 × Table

Let's start learning our times tables. We will begin with our 10 x table.

$1 \times 10 = 10$

$2 \times 10 = 20$

$3 \times 10 = 30$

$4 \times 10 = 40$

$5 \times 10 = 50$

$6 \times 10 = 60$

$7 \times 10 = 70$

$8 \times 10 = 80$

$9 \times 10 = 90$

$10 \times 10 = 100$

$11 \times 10 = 110$

$12 \times 10 = 120$

Say each multiplication problem out loud, replacing the "x" symbol with "times," "multiplied by," or "groups of."

Wild, Wild West

Which cowboy belongs to which horse?

2 × Table

Now let's try learning our 2 x table.

$1 \times 2 = 2$

$2 \times 2 = 4$

$3 \times 2 = 6$

$4 \times 2 = 8$

$5 \times 2 = 10$

$6 \times 2 = 12$

$7 \times 2 = 14$

$8 \times 2 = 16$

$9 \times 2 = 18$

$10 \times 2 = 20$

$11 \times 2 = 22$

$12 \times 2 = 24$

Say each multiplication out loud, replacing the "x" symbol with "times," "multiplied by," or "groups of."

Pixie Party

Which number is hidden behind each pixie?

5 × = 10

× 2 = 20

9 × 2 =

Spot the Mistake

Spot the egg that is not needed to match the number sentence.

4 × 2 = 8

+ + + =

5 × Table

Now you're ready for your 5 x table.

$1 \times 5 = 5$

$2 \times 5 = 10$

$3 \times 5 = 15$

$4 \times 5 = 20$

$5 \times 5 = 25$

$6 \times 5 = 30$

$7 \times 5 = 35$

$8 \times 5 = 40$

$9 \times 5 = 45$

$10 \times 5 = 50$

$11 \times 5 = 55$

$12 \times 5 = 60$

Say each multiplication out loud, replacing the "x" symbol with "times," "multiplied by," or "groups of."

Safari Sun

Which animal has the correct answer?

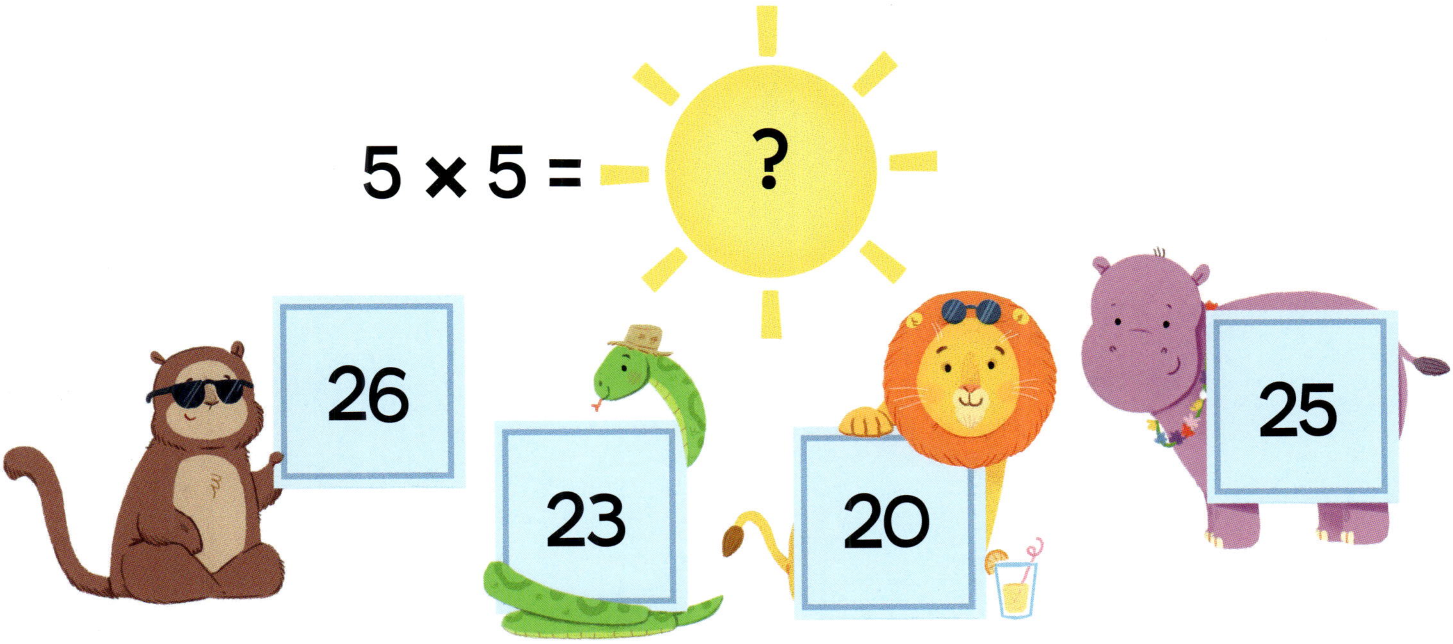

Balloon Brigade

Which numbers are covered by clouds?

Test Your Knowledge

1) 2 x 2 = ?

2) 3 x 2 = ?

3) 4 x 5 = ?

4) 5 x 5 = ?

5) 6 x 10 = ?

6) 7 x 10 = ?

7) 10 x 10 = ?

8) 11 x 10 = ?

9) 12 x 10 = ?

10) 1 x 10 = ?

Multiplication Works Both Ways!

Multiplication is *commutative.* This means that you can swap the numbers you are multiplying and you still get the same answer!

2 x 5 = 10

5 x 2 = 10

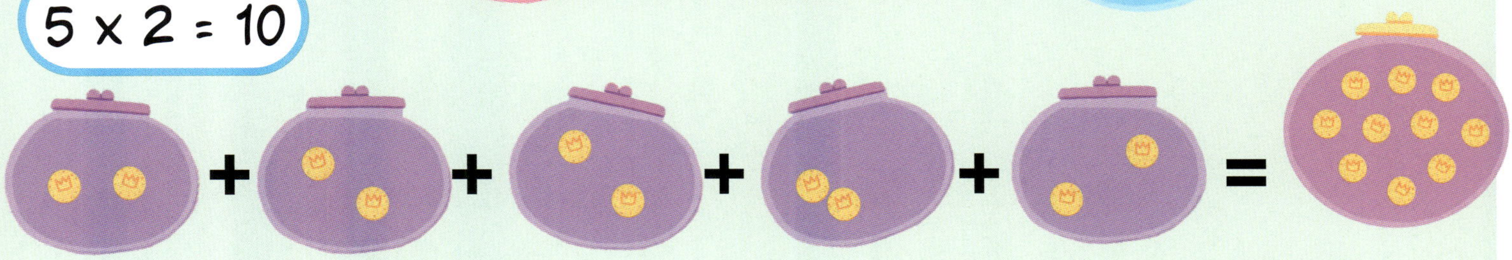

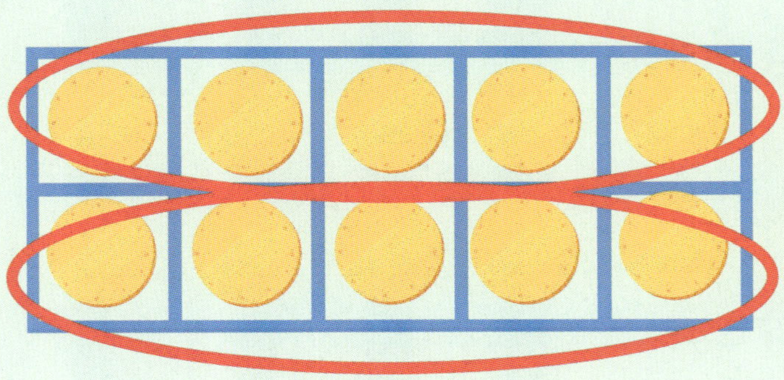

2 x 5 = 10

5 x 2 = 10

Goblin Gruel

Which number is covered by the gruel?

2 × 10 = 20

10 ×  **= 20**

4 × Table

Let's have a look at the 4 x table. If you know your 2 x table, then your 4 x table is no problem. Just *double* your *multiple* from the 2 x table to get the matching multiple in the 4 x table!

1 × 2 = 2   1 × 4 = 4   Double 2 is 4

2 × 2 = 4   2 × 4 = 8   Double 4 is 8

1 × 4 = 4	7 × 4 = 28
2 × 4 = 8	8 × 4 = 32
3 × 4 = 12	9 × 4 = 36
4 × 4 = 16	10 × 4 = 40
5 × 4 = 20	11 × 4 = 44
6 × 4 = 24	12 × 4 = 48

Say each multiplication out loud, replacing the "x" symbol with "times," "multiplied by," or "groups of."

A *multiple* is a number you get when you multiply two numbers together, e.g. the multiple of 2 x 4 is 8. There are two 4s in 8 and four 2s.

Can you think of a multiple of 5?

Dino Dinner

Write the multiplication problem that matches the picture and work out how many dinosaurs are coming to dinner!

$$3 \times ? = ?$$

Under the Sea

Help the crab find the right shell by solving the multiplication.

8 × Table

If you know your 4 x table, then the 8 x table is easy. Just *double* your *multiple* from the 4 x table to get the matching multiple in the 8 x table!

1 × 4 = 4 1 × 8 = 8 **Double** 4 **is** 8

2 × 4 = 8 2 × 8 = 16 **Double** 8 **is** 16

1 × 8 = 8	7 × 8 = 56
2 × 8 = 16	8 × 8 = 64
3 × 8 = 24	9 × 8 = 72
4 × 8 = 32	10 × 8 = 80
5 × 8 = 40	11 × 8 = 88
6 × 8 = 48	12 × 8 = 96

Say each multiplication out loud, replacing the "x" symbol with "times," "multiplied by," or "groups of."

Awesome Ants

Complete the multiplication problem by picking the right ant.

5	×	?	=	40

Fairy Fun

On a piece of paper, draw the correct numbers of fairies and figure out the answer.

$$4 \times 4 = ?$$

3 × Table

Wow! You've already learned your 2, 4, 5, 8, and 10 x tables.
Next up is the 3 x table!

1 × 3 = 3

2 × 3 = 6

3 × 3 = 9

4 × 3 = 12

5 × 3 = 15

6 × 3 = 18

7 × 3 = 21

8 × 3 = 24

9 × 3 = 27

10 × 3 = 30

11 × 3 = 33

12 × 3 = 36

Say each multiplication out loud, replacing the "x" symbol with "times," "multiplied by," or "groups of."

Brick Buildup

Pick the correct brick to fill the space and complete the multiplication.

?

3 3 3 3

12

15

21

25

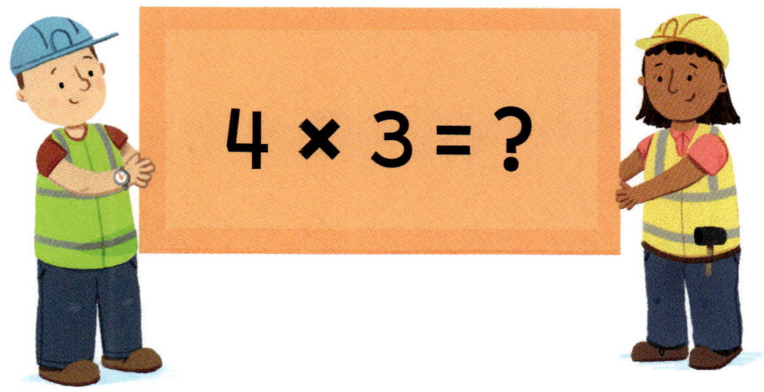

Lost in Space!

Pick the right alien for each spaceship.

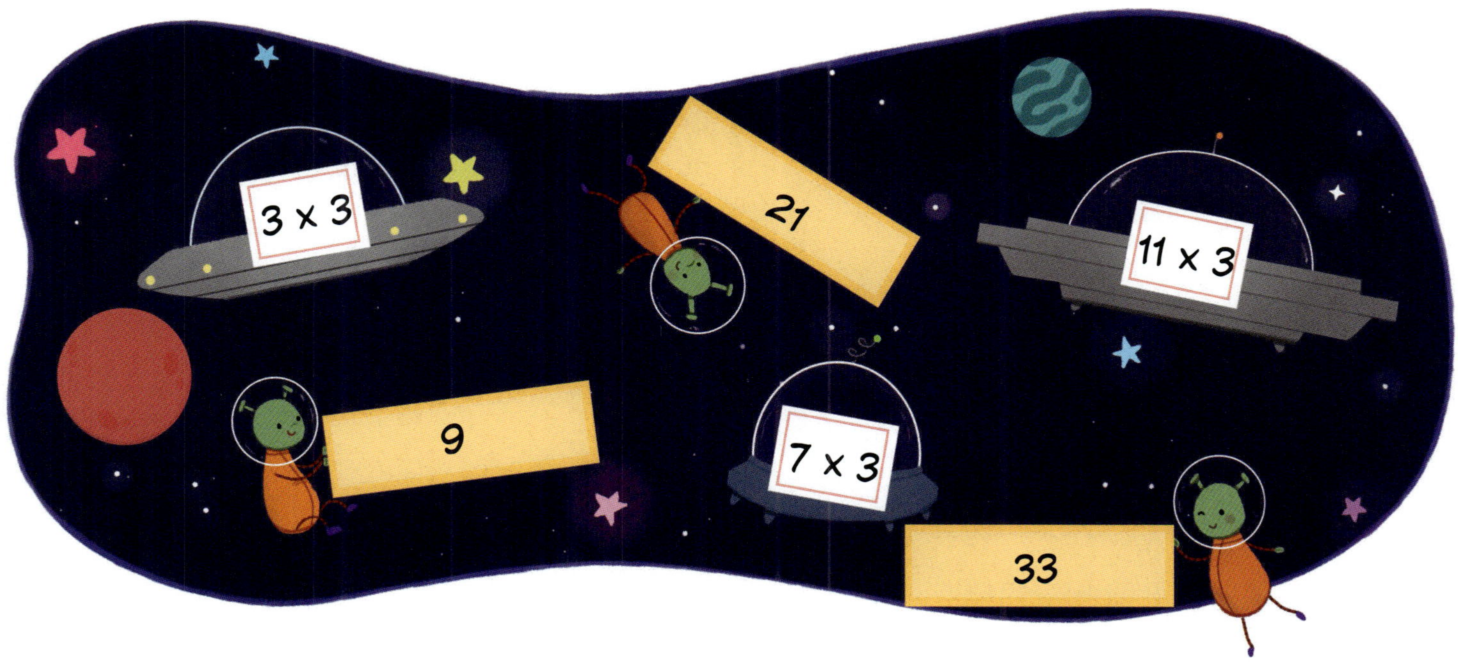

6 × Table

Now let's give the 6 x table a try. If you know the 3 x table, just *double a multiple* from the 3 x table to get the matching multiple in the 6 x table!

1 × 3 = 3 | 1 × 6 = 6 | Double 3 is 6

2 × 3 = 6 | 2 × 6 = 12 | Double 6 is 12

1 × 6 = 6	7 × 6 = 42
2 × 6 = 12	8 × 6 = 48
3 × 6 = 18	9 × 6 = 54
4 × 6 = 24	10 × 6 = 60
5 × 6 = 30	11 × 6 = 66
6 × 6 = 36	12 × 6 = 72

Say each multiplication out loud, replacing the "x" symbol with "times," "multiplied by," or "groups of."

Pirate Pizza Party

Which pizza was ordered by which pirate? Write down each equation.

Busy Bees

Which numbers are the bees hiding?

9 × Table

Now we're ready for the 9 x table. For this one, it's useful to use the 10 x table and then subtract one group of the number.

1 × 9 = 9

2 × 9 = 18

3 × 9 = 27

4 × 9 = 36

5 × 9 = 45

6 × 9 = 54

7 × 9 = 63

8 × 9 = 72

9 × 9 = 81

10 × 9 = 90

11 × 9 = 99

12 × 9 = 108

Say each multiplication out loud, replacing the "x" symbol with "times," "multiplied by," or "groups of."

Spot the Dots

Which times table fact does the second group of giraffes show?
Count the dots!

Pyramid Puzzle

Use the mummy's clue to work out which tomb the explorer should visit.

7 × Table

Some people think the 7 x table is hard, but the truth is you've already come across lots of multiples in it. You've done the hard work already!

$1 \times 7 = 7$

$2 \times 7 = 14$

$3 \times 7 = 21$

$4 \times 7 = 28$

$5 \times 7 = 35$

$6 \times 7 = 42$

$7 \times 7 = 49$

$8 \times 7 = 56$

$9 \times 7 = 63$

$10 \times 7 = 70$

$11 \times 7 = 77$

$12 \times 7 = 84$

Say each multiplication out loud, replacing the "x" symbol with "times," "multiplied by," or "groups of."

Shell Game

This tower follows the 7 x table. Who should go on top?

Penguin Picnic

Figure out what times table fact the second picnic shows.

$7 \times 3 = 21$

$? \times ? = 21$

11 × Table

The 11 x table has a helpful pattern up until 9 x 11.

1 × 11 = 11

2 × 11 = 22

3 × 11 = 33

CAN YOU SPOT THE PATTERN?

1 × 11 = 11

2 × 11 = 22

3 × 11 = 33

4 × 11 = 44

5 × 11 = 55

6 × 11 = 66

7 × 11 = 77

8 × 11 = 88

9 × 11 = 99

10 × 11 = 110

11 × 11 = 121

12 × 11 = 132

Say each multiplication out loud, replacing the "x" symbol with "times," "multiplied by," or "groups of."

Laundry Sort-out

Figure out which item of clothing is the odd one out on each washing line.

Test Your Knowledge

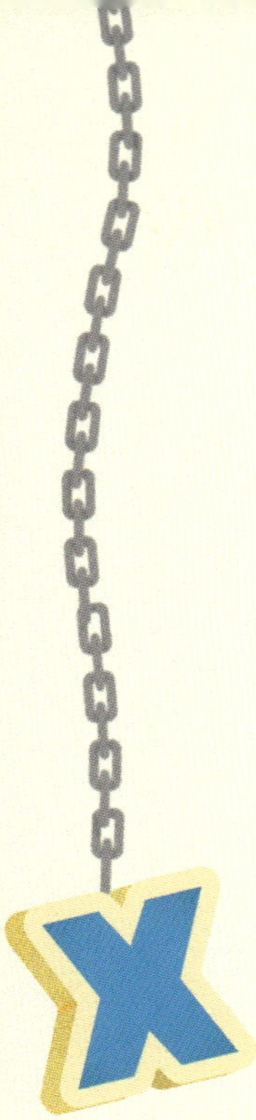

1) 12 x 2 = ?

2) 2 x 6 = ?

3) 2 x 3 = ?

4) 4 x 11 = ?

5) 4 x 6 = ?

6) 4 x 3 = ?

7) 9 x 10 = ?

8) 9 x 9 = ?

9) 8 x 7 = ?

10) 7 x 8 = ?

Test Your Knowledge

1) 3 x 11 = ?

2) 9 x 8 = ?

3) 12 x 10 = ?

4) 3 x 8 = ?

5) 7 x 7 = ?

6) 6 x 7 = ?

7) 4 x 8 = ?

8) 3 x 10 = ?

9) 9 x 11 = ?

10) 8 x 8 = ?

Solutions

Page 5

4 ⊗ 2 ⊜ 8   3 ⊗ 2 ⊜ 6

Page 5

MULTIPLICATION	OTHER
1 Multiplied by	1 Divided by
2 Times	2 Minus
3 Groups of	3 Plus

Page 7

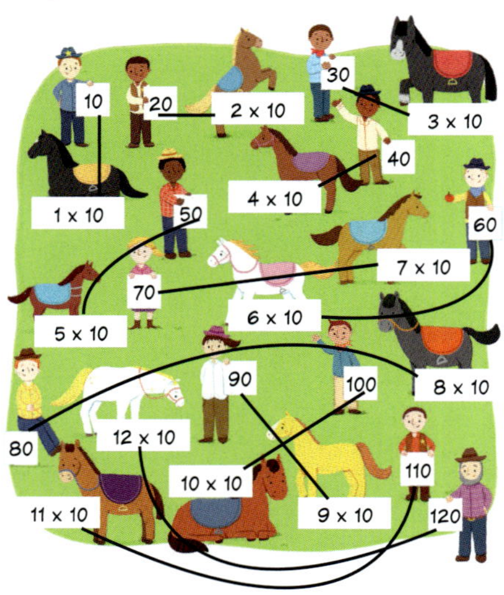

Page 9

5 × (2) = 10   9 × 2 = (18)

(10) × 2 = 20

Page 9

Page 11

Page 11

3 × 5 = (15)   (10) × 5 = 50

8 × (5) = 40

Page 12

1) 4
2) 6
3) 20
4) 25
5) 60
6) 70
7) 100
8) 110
9) 120
10) 10

Page 13

10 X (2) = 20

Page 15

3 × (4) = (12)

Page 15

6 × 4 = 24

Page 17

5 × (8) = 40

Page 17

4 × 4 = 16

Solutions

Page 19

4 × 3 = (12)

Page 19

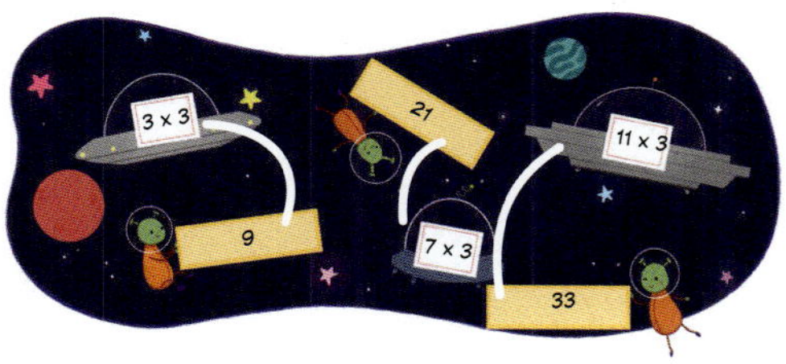

Page 21

Page 21

3 × 9 = (27)   (6) × 5 = 30

2 × (7) = 14

Page 23

(9) × (3) = 27

Page 23

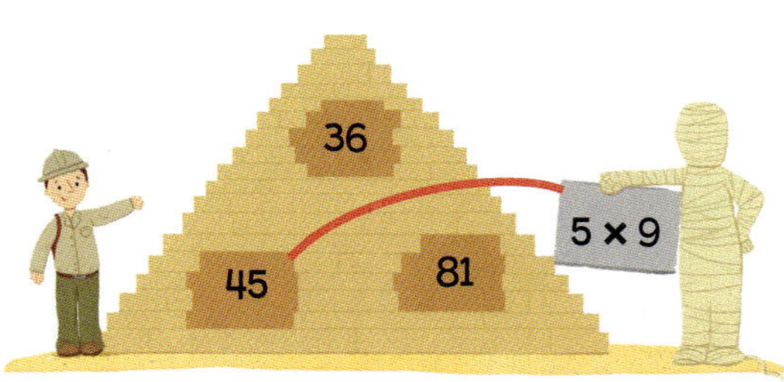

Page 25

28

Page 25

3 × 7 = 21

Page 27

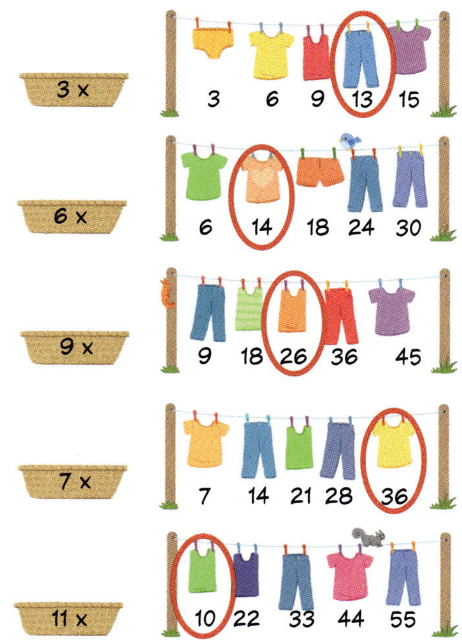

Page 28

1) 24
2) 12
3) 6
4) 44
5) 24
6) 12
7) 90
8) 81
9) 56
10) 56

Page 29

1) 33
2) 72
3) 120
4) 24
5) 49
6) 42
7) 32
8) 30
9) 99
10) 64

Glossary

commutative When numbers being multiplied with each other can be swapped and the answer remains the same.

double Two times the same number.

multiple The answer you get when you multiply two numbers is called the multiple. For example, in 2 x 3 = 6, the multiple is 6.

pattern An ordered set of numbers or shapes that follows one or more rules.

subtract To take away one number from another. Subtraction is expressed using the "minus" symbol (–).

Further Information

Bryan, Lara. *Lift-the-Flap Multiplying and Dividing.* London, UK: Usborne Publishing, 2019.

Marx, Jonny, and John Bigwood. *Sherlock Bones and the Times Table Adventure.* New York, NY: Flash Kids (Sterling Publishing), 2018.

Index